a portrait of oregon

a portrait of oregon

Edited by Robert B. Pamplin, Jr.

Paintings—Howard Snapp
Photographs—Robert Reynolds
Text—Thomas K. Worcester

An OMSI PRESS publication
Oregon Museum of Science and Industry

Distributed by
The Touchstone Press
P.O. Box 81
Beaverton, Oregon 97005

I.S.B.N. Number 0-911518-22-3
Library of Congress Catalog Card No. 73-86802

INTRODUCTION:

Many different cultures have existed through the ages, and to a large extent these contrasting ways of life were dependent on nature. As the natural surroundings cast the medium, so its influence moulded the civilization. Hence, the ambience created by a culture was swayed by gifts nature lent it.

Glancing back into the past, wallowing in the spirit of a bygone time and place, gives you the opportunity to savor some of the good and bad of those times. Or maybe just sitting back and admiring the tenor of the present will inspire a respect and gratitude for those values. The Old West, for instance, offered an array of natural pleasures—vast open land, unusual rock formations and abundant wild game. But, the elements were punishing, and those who survived were indeed hardy. But the land mirrored a stubborn and noble strength causing its inhabitants to cling to its mighty freedom. The New West retains many of these characteristics. The land still has its rugged beauty and the people are still sturdy and independent. And their artificial environment is enhanced by the natural surroundings.

The essence of nature and how it shapes a culture and a people has been the inspiration of *A Portrait of Oregon*. Such an endeavor had to be inspired because it takes a feeling that transcends merely putting together a project to capture the soul of something. Proper to this relation, talents of individuals living in Oregon were chosen. Men who have experienced first-hand what it means to "live Oregon." The photographs of Bob Reynolds bring to your attention a visual acquaintance common to everyone, while the paintings and drawings of Howard Snapp go beyond by bringing to light the country's mood . . . temper . . . humor . . . fire. And Tom Worcester's description of the people and their land adds another dimension to the usual perspective.

Their Oregon provides a way of life virtually unequaled in the world. It offers the physical wonders of snow-capped mountains, sandy beaches, a rich, verdant flora west of the Cascades and a semidesert, "old west" flavor eastward. The undulating Willamette Valley is the scene of choice fertile farms while Eastern Oregon is sagebrush, a faint scent of juniper, and craggy forms of rimrock. All these characteristics join to make Oregon truly a unique experience for any person, native or visitor.

R.B.P., Jr.

Hank Vaughn was a gambler with the pasteboards and the six gun, and more than once he let a man get the draw on him, only to finish his opponent with a flurry of lead slugs.

But Vaughn's most famous gun fight lurches through history, told and retold, with names and places changed as "eye-witnesses" include themselves at the scene of the battle. Some say it was against Sagebrush Brown at The Dalles, while others claim the fight was with Bill Singleton at Sprague. A third and widely accepted version locates the fight in a saloon in Prineville, where Hank may have tried to palm an ace, as he was wont to do in a card game.

According to one reporter, John W. Kelly, a gunman named Charley Long was just as tough as Hank, and considered himself as good with the handgun. Charley challenged Hank, and Hank tossed a large silk handkerchief on the bar. He told Charley to take hold of a corner. As they stretched the silk between them spectators cleared the area and the bartender protested their determination to use his place as a shooting gallery.

On signal, both men drew and fired, each emptying his gun at the other. Four of Charley's shots hit Hank, while Long received a like number of wounds. With empty guns smoking, the two slipped to the floor. But that was not the end. As blood flowed from the punctured bodies, they crawled to each other and pounded first with gun butts, then with fists. Finally they fell back, exhausted, and the crowd waited for their certain death.

But Hank Vaughn struggled mightily, and raised himself enough to shake a fist at Charley and mutter:

"Bet you five dollars you die first!"

"I'll see you and raise you five," coughed Charley, blood in his throat.

Oddly, both men recovered from their multiple wounds. Charley Long was killed in a fight over a water hole, while the notorious Hank Vaughn, gambler, gunman, died in a fall from a horse.

First just a trickle, then the trickle became a flow as hundreds of men, women and children moved across the plains to the promised land at the end of the longest wagon road in history. At Independence, Missouri, the trail branched away from the Old Sante Fe Trail, and the sod busters and settlers headed north, passing rivers and towns and landmarks that became familiar in the history books: North Platte, Chimney Rock, Fort Laramie, Independence Rock, South Pass, Soda Springs, Fort Hall, and Snake. Now they were in Oregon, tired, forlorn, hungry, often with only the dream of the fecund Willamette Valley to keep them moving. Sometimes the last few hundred miles were covered with the family cow and a saddle horse pulling the wagon that had been drawn by a hitch of oxen. At last the Columbia, then The Dalles, end of the Oregon Trail, but not the end of the journey for most of the bone-weary pioneers. Barge or Barlow, they continued into the valley, where the tall grass was inviting, the soil rich for planting, and trees enough to last forever.

It was on to Oregon, and a spirit seldom equalled in the transition of man.

By the millions they fly to Oregon, enroute to their southern vacation quarters, landing in the marshes and fields for a needed rest and feed. Teal, snow geese, mallard, hooded merganser, wood duck, loon, gadwell, redhead, shoveler, canvasback, pintail, Canada goose—all are common in the migratory bird areas east and west of the Cascades. Oregon—a birdwatcher's delight, a hunter's paradise.

He was a character that time had passed by. In fringed buckskins and broad-brimmed hat, with a shaggy head of hair and a long, greying beard, Rattlesnake Pete was right out of the story books of the Old West.

Rattlesnake Pete—or Miles Henry Jackson, as he was christened—landed in Klamath Falls in the middle 1930s with the avowed purpose of becoming a character, and from then on he lived a role that added color to this southern Oregon town.

Pete was armed with two .44 caliber pistols—one a Colt, the other a nickel-plated Merwin-Hulbert, both collector's items. He loaded the guns with blanks, but more than once an unsuspecting visitor to Klamath Falls hit the dust when Pete decided to clear the streets.

On his horse, Old Paint, Pete was an attraction at many parades and festivals, but it was on the streets of Klamath Falls, or at the baseball games which he loved, that Pete made his presence known. The .44s made that easy.

Klamath Falls has been a lot quieter since Pete died in 1966, at the age of 93. But something important is gone.

Many characters have left an indelible imprint in the folklore of Oregon, but perhaps none is more colorful than William W. Brown, a scholarly stockman, who at the turn of the century controlled 136,000 acres of prime grazing land in four counties.

Bill Brown ran both horses and sheep in central Oregon, and nobody, least of all him, knew for sure just how many head he had at any given time. He was known to herd up to 3,000 sheep by himself in order to save the herder's fee, but he also said:

"Herding sheep gives a man a lot of time for reading worthwhile books and doing worthwhile thinking."

Many stories still circulate about Bill Brown, such as his penchant for writing checks on wood chips or soup can labels and his riding horseback in stocking feet to save his boots. He was considered a little strange around Burns and Prineville, because he reportedly never drank, never smoked, never told lies, and never used profane language. One old-timer explained:

"Ol' Bill never married, either. That's why he never had no need for drinkin', smokin', lyin', and swearin'."

When Gov. Oswald West was going to attend the western governors' meeting at Boise in 1912, he rode a black mare from Salem to Idaho. He decided to go by way of Wagontire so that he could meet Bill Brown, already a legend. The rancher was cutting hay when the governor arrived. Gov. West later wrote:

"Upon my arrival, Bill halted his mowing outfit and acknowledged my introduction. The fact that he was about to entertain the governor of his state made little or no impression on the old stockman. However, he agreed to my spending the night at Wagontire."

Bill had one bed at the ranch, which he shared with Gov. West. It was July, and hot, and Bill slept in the same long-handled red flannels that he had been wearing for haying.

The next morning, when Gov. West was preparing to leave, his host presented him with a bill: 50¢ for the supper, 50¢ for breakfast, 50¢ for the bed, and 50¢ for boarding the mare.

Now *there* was a man who knew how to entertain politicians.

The fire was stoked, and the wash tub in place on the cast-iron stove. Annie had poured in three buckets of water, and needed a fourth for the family wash. How many times had she turned the handle—fifteen, sixteen, seventeen. At last the bucket was up, bobbing slightly at the end of the frayed rope. She leaned over the well, caught the bucket, and pulled it to her with thin arms barely able to lift its weight. Annie rested the bucket at the edge of the well, then strained again to hoist it over the side and to the ground. Her young muscles quivered as she straightened up once again, relaxing. From a distance she could hear the *whonk* of the axe as her father attacked yet another tree. Slowly, with both hands, she lifted the bucket and scuffed toward the cabin, taking tiny steps to avoid spilling the precious liquid. At the door she rested once more, wiping sore hands on the wrinkled calico, catching back a wisp of hair. She glanced across the field past the rough-hewn fences, beyond the smoldering stumps, to a small clearing marked by a crude white cross.

"We'll make it," she said. "We have to—that's what Mother wanted."

Like firepits for a modern Paul Bunyan, wigwam burners, remnants of a passing technology, sit decaying, perhaps someday to baffle archaeologists of another era.

Spring splashes a myriad of greens in the Columbia River Gorge: the light shades of maple and alder, darkening with dogwood and fern, deepening to the hues of the Douglas fir, hemlock, and other evergreens.

The Gorge is inviting in its summer cool and its winter romance and intrigue. It can be exciting and challenging, but also refreshing and enchanting.

Once the waterway for explorers, the commerce center for Indians, and a barrier for pioneers, the Columbia River now is virtually a series of lakes behind dams that have stemmed its vibrant flow. But the Columbia is so rich in legend and so important to the founding of Oregon that it must be considered the northwest's highway of history.

It is fall in Oregon. On the coast, the shortened days bring signs of "wintering in" to the human and animal residents who will be there when January storms unleash nature's harshness. In the Columbia River Gorge, a gentle mist settles on the ridgetops and breathes moisture into the valley below. Snow—a blanketing peace to earth—seeks the upper reaches of the Wallowas, driving the deer and elk to lower havens. In central Oregon, nights are cold and clear and the nocturnal yowl of a coyote touches off endless wanderings of the mind. On Willamette Pass, vine maple and alder join other flora to emblazon the hillsides with rich hues of yellow, gold, red, orange and brown. In Lakeview, a falling cottonwood leaf twirls through patches of sunlight and shadow, catches an updraft for a wild moment, then quietly caresses earth.

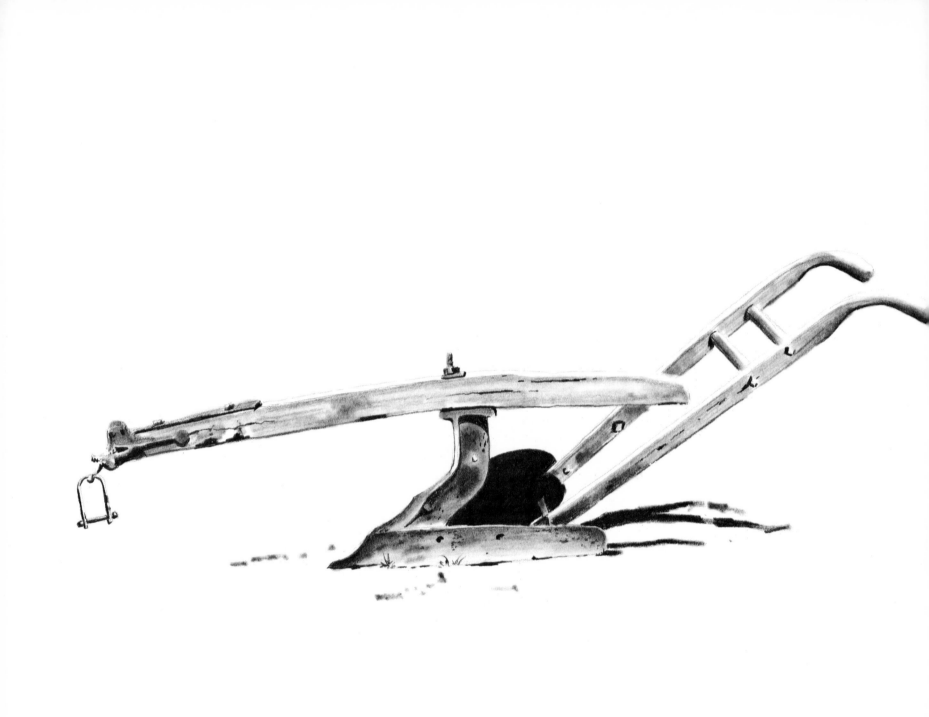

Spring flowers open
To a warming sun that
Chases away the rain.

Clint Spriggs was a horseshoer for 60 years in Cottage Grove before he decided to retire and take life easy.

Not a farrier. As Clint says:

"Everybody was 'horseshoer' then—nobody'd know what you were talking about if you said farrier."

Clint Spriggs is the kind of Oregonian born of independence and bred to work hard. He began his apprenticeship in Ashland at the age of 15, working for 50 cents a day. A blacksmith in Talent offered him more money, so Clint worked there and with his brother in Coburg before moving to Eugene and the shop of Tim Finnigan. When a father-son horseshoeing team moved to Eugene, they claimed that the son was the fastest shoer around. One day Tim Finnigan said:

"Clint, I told that fellow I had $100 that says his boy isn't the fastest shoer in town."

Clint said: "O.K., Tim, that's a good bet. I'll take half of it. You can beat him."

"Heck, Clint, you're not betting on me! I'm betting on you!"

Clint not only won the bet, but was the first shoer in Eugene to make $3.00 a day, big money in those days. Now a farrier gets at least $3.00 a hoof! And when Clint moved to Cottage Grove in April, 1909, some of his patrons still brought their horses from Eugene for him to take care of them.

Today, Clint Spriggs says, "Takes more knowledge than a lot of people believe to be a horseshoer."

And with a knowing smile, he adds: "Guess it just takes common horse sense, too."

Darkness in daylight—
A changing weather.
Now it is raining.

To be in Oregon is to be outdoors. Here is where a fickle Pacific surf scrubs an agate-littered beach, curling, waiting. Here is where skis whisper across powder snow at Mt. Bachelor. Here is where on any weekend in the summer the truck campers cross the Cascades like a string of migrating snails.

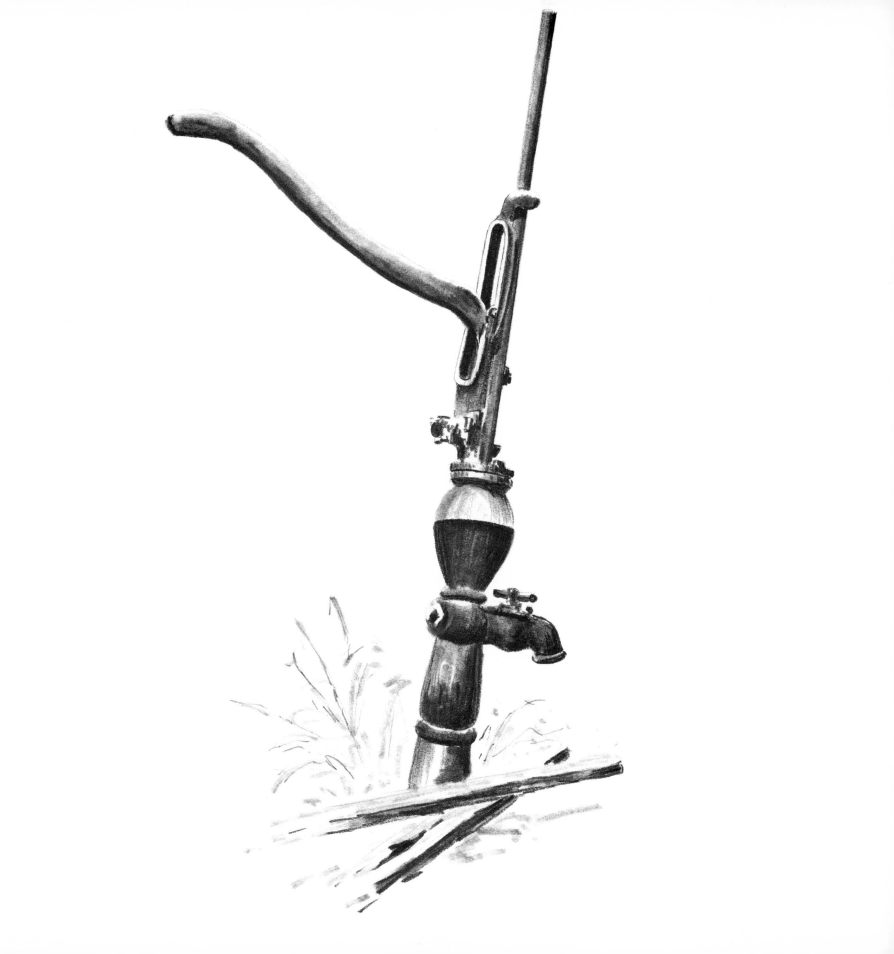

"It does not rain in Oregon, but now and then we have heavy mist."

"It does not rain in Oregon. Just low clouds."

"It does not rain in Oregon. We have a high dew line."

"It does not rain in Oregon. Occasionally the spray blows in from the ocean."

"It DOES NOT rain in Oregon. But . . ."

Not all of Oregon's early ministries took place in an established place of worship. Witness Pulpit Rock at The Dalles, or the circuit riding preachers of Roseburg and Medford.

But one of the most resourceful evangelists was the Reverend Mr. G. W. Hall, pastor of the Baptist Church in Coos Bay. When the Rev. Mr. Hall arrived in Coos Bay in 1910, he said:

"This is glorious country, but how do I reach the people with my ministry? So many live on the shores or up the rivers where there are no roads. They travel only by boat and cannot attend church on Sunday unless the tide is right."

But the pastor found the solution himself:

"If I can't get the people to church, then I shall take the church to the people."

And so, with funds raised by subscription from the membership, the Rev. Mr. Hall acquired a boat, a seaworthy craft, but capable of operating in shallow water. Perhaps its most unusual characteristic was its chapel, complete with pump organ. The boat was christened "The Lifeline" and each Sunday, the Rev. Mr. Hall (or the Rev. Captain Hall) would make a circuit of Coos Bay, nosing into inlets and logging docks to pick up churchgoers. The meetings usually were held in a home, but if the tide was too low to reach shore easily, the minister would drop anchor and deliver the services in the chapel, with Mrs. Hall playing hymns on the organ.

"The Lifeline" was used for Sunday school, too, and occasionally for a funeral or a wedding. Social gatherings by the congregation also were held on board. But after a few years, as more roads were cut into areas formerly isolated, fewer persons attended church on the floating chapel.

The Lifeline passed into obscurity in 1912, having served its purpose in an unusual work of the Lord and the man who made it so.

"When tillage begins, other arts follow. The farmers therefore are the founders of human civilization."

Daniel Webster

"And I'm going to buy silk shirts and white ties, and a long, frock coat like the gamblers wear, and I'll have a house in San Francisco, with maids and a butler, and linen table cloths and sterling silver, and I'll eat Alaskan crab and Russian caviar and drink French wines, and I'll travel to Europe and the Orient, and I'll bring back gem stones and furs for beautiful women. What'll *you* do when we hit pay dirt, Frank?"

Elijah Coalman was more than the dean of the Mt. Hood climbers. He was embodiment of the mountain's soul.

Born in its shadow and reared on its slopes, Lige Coalman knew and loved Mt. Hood from the time he could remember. He made his first ascent in 1896 at the age of 15, and from then until an accident slowed him in 1917 he climbed the mountain 586 times for pay and for pleasure. More than once his life was endangered—a fall into a crevasse, a slide on a glacier, a shower of falling rock—but for Lige that was normal to being part of the mountain. Once he climbed from Timberline to the summit in 96 minutes, a feat that usually takes even experienced mountaineers five to six hours.

Lige lived several summers alone at the top of the mountain in a summit cabin he built while serving as a fire lookout. From this snowclad belvedere he sometimes was the first to see climbers in danger, and is credited personally with saving the lives of five injured persons.

Above all, Lige Coalman respected the mountain, knew its moods and whims, and adjusted his symbiotic life accordingly.

Near the crest of McKenzie Pass, in west central Oregon, is a monument to the courage and endeavor of a man who had the foresight to see the need for a road over the Cascades, linking the high, wide spaces of Central Oregon with the fertile Willamette Valley. Using simple hand tools, and often working alone, John Templeton Craig spent several years of his life hacking out a wagon road over the pass. Craig was told:

"You're a fool to waste your time on a road through those mountains. Nobody'll use it. You've been at it two years now—if you spent the same time on your farm, you'd have the finest place in Lane County."

Some thought Craig was demented, others humored him, grubstaking him when needed, and occasionally helping with the wagon road.

Craig built a cabin on McKenzie Pass in 1860, and lived there while working on his road. It also served as a shelter in later years when he carried the mail over the pass on snowshoes from Eugene to Camp Polk, near Sisters in central Oregon. An exceptionally high chimney allowed him to find the cabin even when the snow was 10 feet deep on the pass.

Near Christmas, 1877, John T. Craig left the Willamette Valley in a blizzard to make the mail run to Camp Polk. His frozen body was found several weeks later in his cabin. Nearby were life-saving matches that showed all signs of having been wet at the time their user tried to strike them.

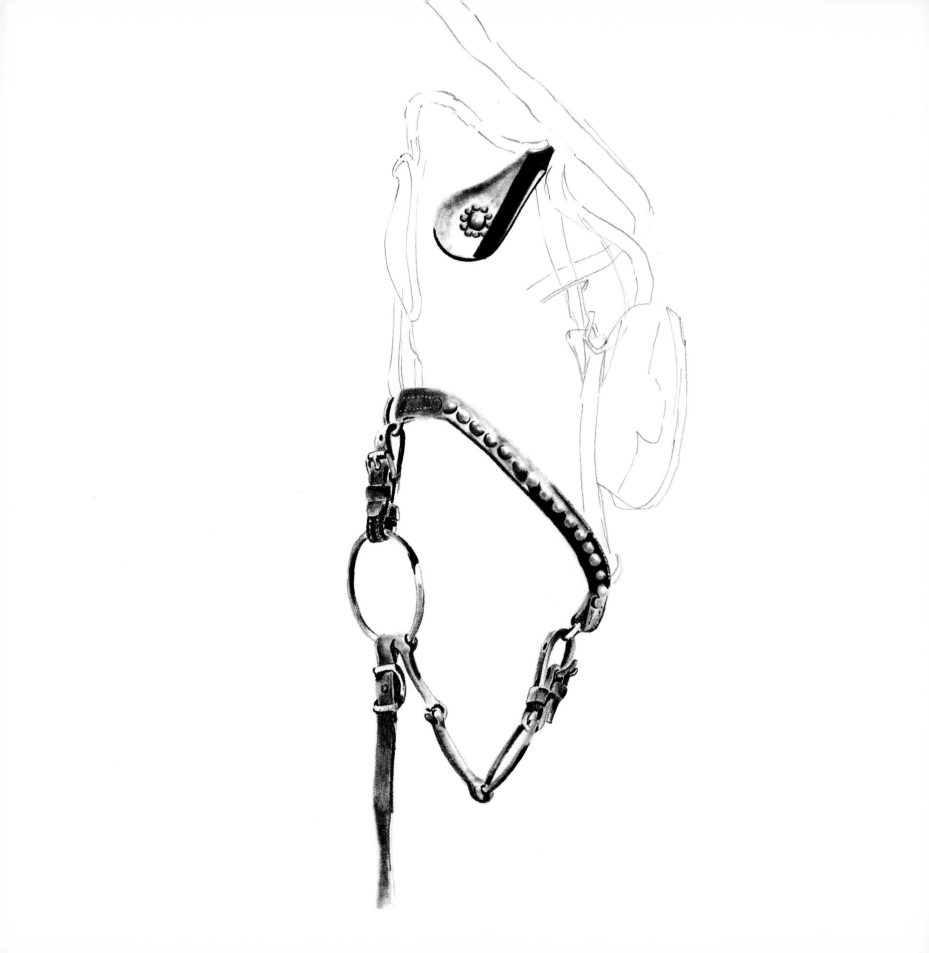

When General Crook retired in 1900 he was well past the average age for his kin. He was known by every elderly resident of the Goose Lake Valley, and in his youth he is said to have outrun everything on the road. General, you see, was the prize trotting horse of C. U. Snider, of Lakeview, and while active in the harness he travelled most of Oregon, California, and Nevada.

Even after he retired General lived an active and interesting life, meandering through Lakeview on his daily walk, visiting friendly merchants for a snack of sugar or apple. So when he died, it was almost a day of mourning in the town.

General died July 31, 1906, at the age of 38, then Oregon's oldest horse. He was buried with full honors befitting his rank in the southeast corner of the courthouse square in Lakeview. And the Lake County Examiner opined:

"No useless coffin enclosed his breast nor in sheet nor shroud we wound him."

Five men—Joseph Field, William Bratton, George Gibson and two others named Willard and Wiser—left a monument in Oregon history that was lost for nearly a century even though situated in one of the state's most popular beach towns.

The five were members of the Lewis and Clark party, and their contribution to the welfare of the expedition during the winter the explorers spent in Oregon was 15 to 20 pounds of salt, a preservative desperately needed for the cross country journey back to a cache of provisions at the headwaters of the Missouri.

Using stones found at the site, and a clay mud from the nearby Necanicum River, the five men, with assistance from friendly Clatsop Indians, constructed a cone-shaped hut, roughly eight feet in diameter. Several openings in the walls of the hut served as flues. Here, the Pacific brine boiled in large iron kettles, and the residual salt was collected and stored. Between January 6 and February 20, 1806, the saltmakers distilled out nearly 20 pounds of salt which they delivered to the main party of the expedition, 15 miles north at Ft. Clatsop.

Captain Meriwether Lewis's response to their efforts is recorded in his journal:

"The salt was a great treat to myself and most of the party—I say most of the party because my friends Capt. Clark declares it to be a mere matter of indifference to him whether he uses it (salt) or not; for myself I must confess I felt a considerable inconvenience from the want of it; the want of bread, I considered trivial provided I get fat meat, for as to the species of meat I am not particular: the flesh of the dog, the horse, and the wolf, having from habit become equally familiar (as) with any other and I have learned to think that if the chord be sufficiently strong, which binds the soul and body together, it does not much matter about the materials which compose it."

"The story of the toilsome march of the wagon trains over the plains will be received by the future generations almost as a legend on the borderland of myth, rather than as veritable history. It will be accepted, indeed, but scarcely understood. Even now to the survivors who made the journey the realities of it seem half fabulous. It no longer has the appearance of a rational undertaking. Rapid transit of the present time seems almost to relegate the story to the land of the fable. No longer can we understand the motives that urged our pioneers toward the indefinite horizon that seemed to verge on the unknown. Looking back on the movement now, a mystery appears in it. It was the final effort of that profound impulse which, from a time far preceding the dawn of history, has pushed the race to which we belong to discovery and occupation of western lands."

Harvey W. Scott
1904

"Those who wish to change the name of Bull Run to Cascade, and Portland to Multnomah, must remember that this idea of changing names is not new . . . Quite likely there are people who would like to change the name of Oregon to something else. And good arguments could be made in behalf of that change—at least as good as some of the arguments made in support of other proposed changes. The name Oregon is said to be of Spanish origin, and why should this country tolerate a name which traces its ancestry to a nation from which we were compelled to take Cuba and the Philippines. Besides, 'Oregon' sounds a great deal like 'Are he gone,' which would be bad English. Then, too, Eastern people who are not familiar with the pronunciation of the word might pronounce it "O'regon," with an Irish sound. If they should do that, it would give offense to our English friends and perhaps prevent our securing a number of desirable additions to our citizenship.

"But that is not all. Other people might call it 'Ore-gon,' which would convey the impression that our mines have been depleted of their wealth. On the whole, this name of ours is open to so many serious objections that it ought to be changed."

Oregonian
October 20, 1907

Reub Long, Oregon's high desert guru, notes: "Most of the West was settled by adventurers, trappers; it was mostly a transient civilization. But Oregon was founded by missionaries and families. Their success was in direct proportion to the loyalty, courage and stamina of our pioneer women. There is a story about a man coming up a trail to a cabin. He watched as the pioneer wife walked into the kitchen and then he saw a cougar jump through the kitchen window. The stranger ran to the husband, who was chopping wood outside:

"I know, I know,' the husband said. 'But I never did like those big cats, and he'll just have to get out of there the best he can'."

Rust blankets the relics of man,
clinging—a living color.

Bill Henley was young and cocky when he arrived in the Jordan Valley from Jacksonville. Bill cut teeth on a saddle horn, and for him, ranching was the only life. Before he died he managed most of the ranches along the Donner and Blitzen River—the Bell A, Double O, P Ranch, Roaring Springs and Rock Creek. He respected his men, and they respected him. And so it was with sadness that a cowboy entered a popular bar in the basement of the general store in the Narrows between Harney and Malheur Lakes and announced:

"Uncle Bill Henley's learned to ride an automobile. What's the country coming to, anyway?"

Bill was as oblivious to roads in his Model T as he was when he rode horseback, and often he boiled out the radiator in a dry wash away from the trail. He never seemed to learn that merely driving a car to water was not enough.

Once when Bill Henley got a new car, a white Buick roadster, he turned it over to a cowboy named Tex to break before he took the wheel.

"Get her gentled out nice and easy, Tex. I don't want the men to know I can't handle her."

Shaniko! A lilting name, the title for a song or a western movie. Look and listen. The years fade away to past generations of pigtailed girls in ruffled ginghams "skinning the cat" in the school yard.

Shaniko! Then the largest inland railhead for sheep in the world. (More than 4,000,000 pounds of wool shipped from the town in 1901)

Shaniko! Once a growing metropolis, to rival the burgeoning cities west of the Cascades. Center of development for all of central Oregon.

Shaniko—a ghost town that refuses to die.

Each fall, when sodden clouds hang heavily over the Willamette Valley, aerial migration often can be witnessed in the evenings. It is then that the yips of winging geese fall to earth-bound romantics who dare not follow. For the geese, Oregon is but a welcome resting station on a long flight. For the Oregonians, the geese are a symbol of a freedom that few possess.

Crows' feet and squint marks were chiseled into the hammered-copper face of the cowboy and steady eyes met the gaze of a stranger openly. His faded jeans, checkered shirt, pointed boots and curl-brimmed straw hat were his uniform, and he stood at the jackpine corral, one foot on a lower rail, as he answered the question with a good-natured patience.

"Travel? Where would I go? This is Oregon —I'm already there."

The old fisherman clasped the oilskin at his throat, and tugged again at the sou'wester to keep it from following the wind. He walked slowly at the edge of the surf watching the running tide and scouring the sands in the endless search of the beachcomber.

He stopped to wipe the water from his glasses, and glanced toward the rocky headland, then down the length of sand in the other direction. He was alone, for this was the kind of day to share only with the gulls.

Then he saw a quick movement at the tide line where a mud-dog was stranded above the water level, flopping, gasping. Slowly, with the care of a loving mother lifting a baby, he picked up the hapless fish and released it in the surf.

"That thing's not even good for bait," he thought, "but nothin' should die that way."

The wind-driven rain, which began as a light mist, now clattered against the slicker, and stung his face like tiny spear points. His lips tasted salty from the spray blowing away from the breakers. Cold, moist air seeped through his clothing, chilling his lean body. He quickened his pace, ducking his chin behind a shoulder to avoid the nipping rain.

Suddenly he was not alone. Another walker approached, head down, searching, like an anxious bird seeking a morsel of food.

They met where a freshet furrowed its way from the bank to the surf. The fisherman spoke first:

"Nice day, ain't it."

"Beautiful, beautiful," the other acknowledged.

He came from California, brash, confident, his knowledge of men and cattle belying his 24 years, driving 1200 head to Oregon, where grass was belly deep to a heifer, and water to wash it down. No fences braced the land then, and the man who controlled it was the man who owned it. Or so Pete French thought.

But settlers were not to be denied their piece of sod, though in classic range-war confrontation, Pete French and other cattlemen tried to keep the land open for grazing. Thus it was only a matter of time before Pete would face a gun.

Friends say Pete always claimed he would be shot. It was merely a question of who would have the honor, for among his enemies—and he had many—killing Pete French was considered of the highest order.

Complex and controversial, French was not a mixer, but he was pleasant and courteous, and exceedingly hospitable. It is said that no traveler ever was refused a meal at his cookhouse. But while he could share his sustenance, he could not share his land. When the valley was opened to homesteading, Pete had his men file claims, which he then bought from them. He also bought out settlers, often finding graphic ways to make the more stubborn landowners listen to his line of reasoning. But one man refused to listen. Ed Oliver. Inevitably it was Oliver who won in the showdown with French, and a single bullet dropped the cattleman from his saddle.

Oliver was acquitted on a plea of self-defense. But what was Pete French defending? The right to open range versus a settler's home, that ironic conflict of the West.

Rivers have been essential to both the transportation and commerce in Oregon. And while the Columbia, named by American sea captain Robert Gray, was the most sought-after as the "Great River of the West," perhaps none was more perplexing to explorers and cartographers than the Willamette, or the "Multnomah" as it was named and known for a brief period after the Lewis and Clark Expedition.

Much credence for a great basin west of the Rocky Mountains and for a mammoth river that drained that basin was given to American, British and Spanish explorers who visited the region in the late 18th and early 19th centuries. Captain William Clark discovered what he thought was that river on the return voyage of the Lewis and Clark trip, and local Indians drew a map for him which greatly distorted the distance drained by the river. This distortion was perpetuated by cartographers of the day who continued to use Clark's rough map as the basis for their maps of the area west of the Rocky Mountains. One of the noted map-makers of the day, John Melish, of Philadelphia, extended the "Multnomah" to the Great Salt Lake, and noted:

"Viewing it in its connection with the headwaters of the Missouri, the la Platte, the Arkansas, and the Rio del Norte it (the Multnomah) deserves particular notice, as it will probably be at no very distant period, the route of overland communication through the interior of Louisiana to the settlements at the mouth of the Columbia River."

As late as 1825 the Multnomah was thought to be several hundred miles long. Finally, a Hudson's Bay Company cartographer, working with information furnished by British explorer Peter Skene Ogden, published maps that refuted the myth created by earlier distortions. Only then did the settlers and the explorers in the beautiful Willamette Valley understand that the legendary Multnomah extended a mere 150 miles from its head in the Oregon Cascades to its confluence with the mighty Columbia.

Twisting, skipping, rising abruptly above the surging waves, the sandpiper scours the Oregon beaches, stopping to feast on morsels the ever-throbbing ocean has readied for him. Now he is at the water's edge, scampering ahead of the foaming surf on stilt-like legs, darting into the water, pecking. Then he is off again in aggravated flight, searching for an avian eldorado.

"The uniform testimony of an intelligent multitude have established the fact that the country in question (Oregon) is the most valuable of all the unoccupied parts of the earth. Its peculiar location and facilities, and physical resources for trade and commerce; its contiguous markets; its salubrity of climate; its fertility of soil; its rich and abundant productions; its extensive forests of valuable timber; and its great water Channel diversifying by its numerous branches the whole country, and spreading canals through every part of it, are sure indications that Providence has designed this last reach of an enlightened emigration to be the residence of a people whose singular advantages will give them unexampled power and prosperity."

Hall Jackson Kelley
1829

Hathaway Jones operated a mule train on the Rogue River, and he packed in mail and supplies to remote settlements on the river. But though Hathaway had a good reputation on the trail, he was better known for his stories. As a friend, Claude Riddle, once wrote:

"Hathaway talked funny. He had something wrong with his palate or nose that impeded his speech. He told me one day that his Pa got quarrelsome and hit him in the nose with a shovel and that was what caused the trouble. He said his father was older than he was at the time."

Hathaway specialized in bear stories. One favorite:

"One time I came around a large rock on the trail, and a big bear reared up right in my face with eyes about as big as a bean. I whupped up Ol' Betsy and shot him clean in the head, but the bear turned around so fast the bullet came back and hit me in the face."

Hathaway was proud of that rifle though. Used to claim he had to shoot salted bullets:

"That rifle would kill game so far away, if you didn't salt the bullets, the meat would spoil before you got there."

Hathaway was a peaceful man all of his life. About the only time he'd get angry was when someone else was credited with telling bigger lies than his. In fact when the *Oregonian* named another man liar of the year, Hathaway threatened to sue for defamation of character.

The death of Hathaway Jones on September 21, 1937 meant the true end of an era, for at the time, Hathaway had the country's only remaining mule train carrying United States mail. Hathaway's horse, Baldy, and the mules came into camp alone that September night. Searchers backtracking the trail found mail and parcels, and eventually the body of the infamous storyteller, broken and lifeless near the trail he had ridden for 16 years. What happened, no one knows, but the elastic mind and silvery tongue of Hathaway Jones were stilled forever.

Sunlight shatters into sparkles and flashes as it touches the dancing waters of the Metolius on a bright June day. Across the river a verdant meadow, sprinkled with wildflowers, stretches to brushy hillocks. Nearby, the towering pines provide a frame for a distant Mt. Jefferson, which stands as a sentinel before the gods of elegance.

Can such beauty be reserved for mere man?

A rodeo cowboy would rather say he won at the Calgary Stampede, Cheyenne Frontier Days, or the Pendleton Round-Up than anywhere else. And Pendleton boasts the roughest, toughest, meanest stock in the country, as well as the finest riders and the fastest pace of the rodeo circuit.

Nobody thinks higher of the cowboys or loves the Round-Up more than Bob Chambers, saddle maker, former bull rider, and the public address announcer for the big show. Chambers knows cowboys and understands their feelings, and is especially careful not to disturb the man in the chute by saying too much about him:

"Just give my name and where I'm from. That's enough."

But Bob does like to boost the beginners, and will not go heavy on the champion. As he says:

"The beginner is taking the same risk and has paid the same money as the champion."

Bob has a simple formula for working a rodeo.

"I try to pick up a crowd when I open the show, and never drop 'em until I'm done. I try to give the color and the lore, so that people can learn to love rodeo the way I do. And if I sense the crowd wondering about something that happened in the arena, I try to explain how it might effect the judging. But I never judge a rodeo on the mike."

Bob Chambers' greatest day was when he rode Fiddle Faddle to the whistle at a Kansas rodeo.

The bull, 1870 pounds of live TNT, had been out four years and never had been ridden the distance. But the bull had the last moment—as Chambers was getting off, the animal hooked him with a horn, breaking the rider's nose.

Pendleton has a sophisticated rodeo audience, and over the years the crowd has seen the great and the near-great of the championship circuit. And how do the riders of yesterday compare with the new breed of cowboy? Bob Chambers says:

"The old-timers couldn't carry the riggin' of these kids today."

That's high praise from one who's been there.

It is said that when Whispering Thompson left Meacham at the top of the Blue Mountains you could hear him clear down in Pendleton on one side and La Grande on the other.

Whispering drove a mule team, and was one of the best-known drivers in the 1870s and 1880s in northeastern Oregon. He liked to talk to himself and to his mules, only when Whispering talked to himself, it was like a bullmoose singing to his cow. But this helped the other drivers on the narrow roads in the Blue Mountains, for they always knew when Thompson was approaching, and they could find a turn-out before having a precipitous meeting.

Thompson once won a bet in Pendleton that he could turn his 14-mule team and long freight wagon around in the intersection of Main and Court Streets. Another time the *East Oregonian* newspaper noted:

"Last Wednesday the flute-like voice of Whispering Thompson could be heard about two miles away. We went to see what was the matter and found his 14-mules in front of a house which had been moved a fourth of a mile in four hours, with Thompson gently encouraging his mules."

The mule skinner has been dead for about 80 years, but even so, when the breeze is gentle in the Blue Mountains, you still can hear a faint "Hi-yup" that the old timers will tell you is a Whispering Thompson echo still resounding off the canyon walls.

With the possible exception of faded barns and lighthouses, none of man's creations evoke more nostalgia than Oregon's covered bridges.

Photographers study the bridges for hours, seeking the proper light and perspective for the perfect picture; artists depict the bridges as representative of a past society; sentimentalists envision the echoing clippity-clop of horse-drawn vehicles passing through its portals; and true bridgophiles drive miles out of their way to see these stanchions of yesterday. But to the travelling Oregonians, the bridges, if not common-place, are a familiar sight to be discovered anew on the secondary roads and bypasses that cross the waterways.

Ethnic influence is evident in various sections of Oregon, and none more prominent than the Spanish terms used in the ranch country of southeastern Oregon. "Rodeo," "sombrero," "riata," "mecarte," all were common, as common as the single-cinch saddle, silver-mounted trappings, and big-roweled spurs of the Mexican *vaqueros* who cowboyed there. With the exception of rodeo, which has become a popular sporting event, the Spanish-Mexican influence did not reach the Blue Mountains or the Columbia River, or cross the Cascades to western Oregon.

"Steamboating" was a common term in the Oregon mining camps and a name frequently applied to a geographical feature in the area, not because a boat propelled by steam power was near the area, but because when a mine played out, or did not meet the expectations of its owner, it was said to have "steamboated." Mining being what it is, many relics of the golden past litter the countryside, now the haven for a varmit or an impromptu bird bath.

Its long, spiked leaves have been used for mats, its roots for nourishment, and its silky down for pillow stuffing. But today the brown, wiener-shaped cattail flower, easily recognized in the swamps and marshes, is a favored decoration in the homes of Oregonians, often complemented by the simplicity of driftwood.

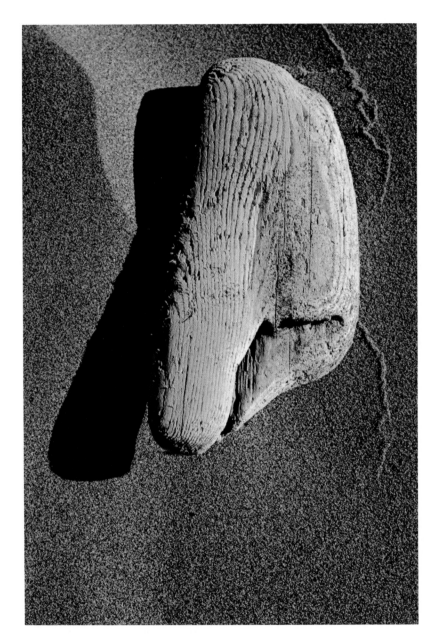

He was only a mite of a lad, and except for the spinning rod he could have stepped out of another century: a freckled-face, shadowed by an aged straw hat, faded blue jeans, bare feet encrusted with a layer of dirt that gives a small boy security, elbows torn out of the shirt. Slowly he cast to the pilings, retrieving the line expertly with a steady wind of the reel. Cast after cast did not produce a strike.

Finally the old man who had been standing on the road, watching quietly as the young angler worked the water, spoke:

"You don't seem to be catching any."

The response was not that of a child, but rather a seasoned philosopher:

"Naw, but it don't matter. Today's a day for fishin', not catchin'."

Life for the professional man in Central Oregon before the turn of the century was almost as rugged as that of the settler or the ranchers. For the doctor, the judge, the dentist or the preacher, the horse and buggy was a necessary conveyance. When a doctor was called to help one of the ranchers far away from the small towns that were beginning to grow on the Oregon desert the need was serious. An accident, a shooting, or complications at birth. A man would ride hard all day and night, changing horses at the various ranches along the way to get the doctor. The physician, then, would drive as fast as his team would go, also changing horses as often as two or three times a trip. For this he charged $1.00 round trip, as well as his regular fee.

Mrs. Horace Belknap, of Prineville, once said: "To be the wife of a country doctor, you can't be jealous. Your husband belongs to the community. He is with families in illness, and comforts them in death. Never plan too much on your husband being able to accompany you anywhere."

How well she knew! The Belknap wedding was delayed half an hour while Horace Belknap tended to the birth of a baby.

On signal by the lookout stationed on a fence or high bush the nervous quail scatter like tourists caught in a sudden rain, first dashing for cover, then whirring into frenzied flight. A choice upland game bird, the quail is at home in the canyons and rimrock of central Oregon and in the thickets and brambles of the western sector of the state.